All-In-One Piano Lessons

Book B

FOREWORD

The **All-In-One Piano Lessons Books A and B** combine selected pages from the Piano Lessons, Technique, Solos, Theory Workbook, and Practice Games into one easy-to-manage book. Upon completion of the **All-In-One Piano Lessons Books A and B,** students will be ready to continue into Level 2 of the **Hal Leonard Student Piano Library.**

When music excites our interest and imagination, we eagerly put our hearts into learning it. The music in the **Hal Leonard Student Piano Library** encourages practice, progress, confidence, and best of all – success! Over 1,000 students and teachers in a nationwide test market responded with enthusiasm to the:

- variety of styles and moods
- natural rhythmic flow, singable melodies and lyrics
- "best ever" teacher accompaniments
- improvisations integrated throughout the **Lesson Books**
- orchestrated accompaniments included in audio and MIDI formats.

When new concepts have an immediate application to the music, the effort it takes to learn these skills seems worth it. Test market teachers and students were especially excited about the:

- "realistic" pacing that challenges without overwhelming
- clear and concise presentation of concepts that allows room for a teacher's individual approach
- uncluttered page layout that keeps the focus on the music.

The **Hal Leonard Student Piano Library** is the result of the efforts of many individuals. We extend our gratitude to all the teachers, students and colleagues who shared their energy and creative input. May this method guide your learning as you bring this music to life.

Best wishes,

Barbara Kreader   Fred Kern   Phillip Keveren   Mona Rejino

Authors
Barbara Kreader, Fred Kern, Phillip Keveren, Mona Rejino

Consultants
Tony Caramia, Bruce Berr, Richard Rejino

Manager, Educational Piano
Jennifer Linn

Editor   *Illustrator*
Anne Wester   Fred Bell

PLAYBACK+
Speed • Pitch • Balance • Loop

To access audio, visit:
www.halleonard.com/mylibrary

Enter Code
4441-9692-7135-3813

ISBN 978-1-4234-8435-6

HAL•LEONARD®

Visit Hal Leonard Online at
www.halleonard.com

Contact us:
Hal Leonard
7777 West Bluemound Road
Milwaukee, WI 53213
Email: info@halleonard.com

In Europe, contact:
Hal Leonard Europe Limited
42 Wigmore Street
Marylebone, London, W1U 2RN
Email: info@halleonardeurope.com

In Australia, contact:
Hal Leonard Australia Pty. Ltd.
4 Lentara Court
Cheltenham, Victoria, 3192 Australia
Email: info@halleonard.com.au

CONTENTS

STEPS

*✓

	Page No.	Audio Tracks

* Students can check pieces as they play them.

SKIPS

*✓

* Students can check pieces as they play them.

LINES AND SPACES

Some notes are written on **lines:**

LINE NOTE

Some notes are written in **spaces:**

SPACE NOTE

Music is written on a **STAFF** of 5 lines and 4 spaces.

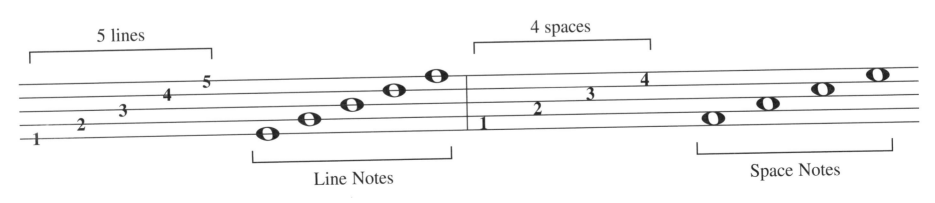

5 lines

4 spaces

Line Notes

Space Notes

Line Note —o— Or Space Note ⊙ ?

Come and play on the line-space jungle gym.

1. Circle each child's face.
   The circle will look like either a line note or a space note.
2. Underline the correct answer.

HOW NOTES MOVE ON THE STAFF

REPEAT

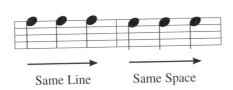

Same Line   Same Space

STEP (2nd)

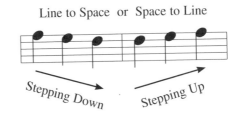

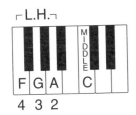

Title:_____

You already know how to play this song.
Do you know its name?

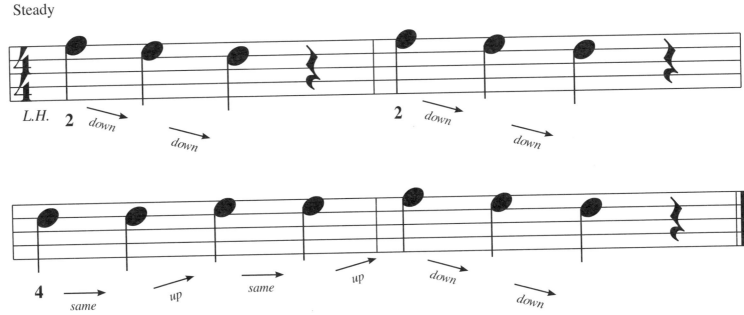

How Notes Move
(Activity Page)
Help Party Cat decorate some balloons for his music party.

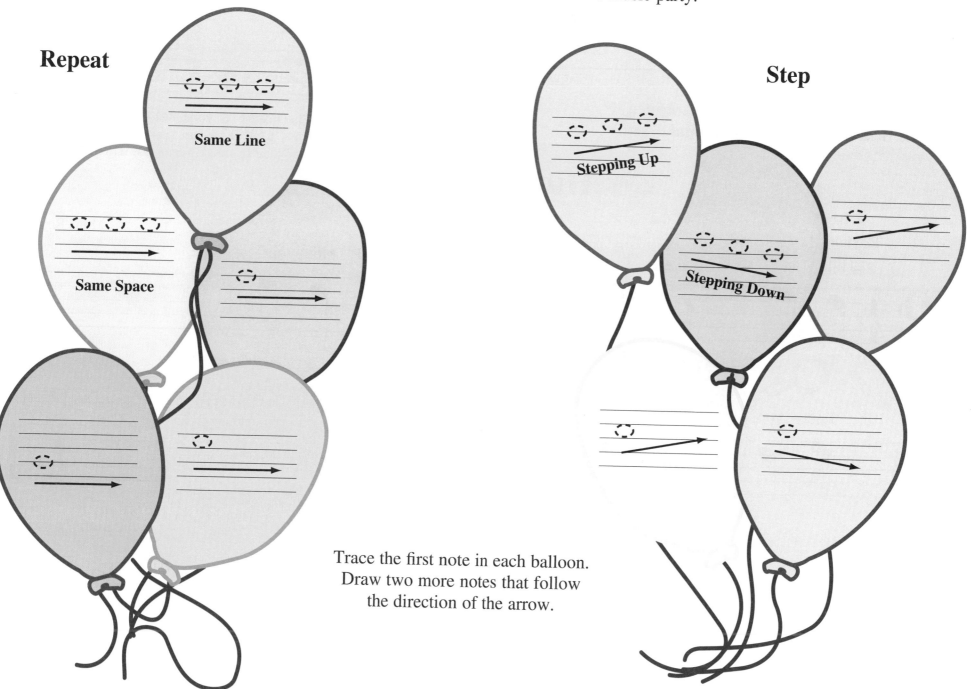

Trace the first note in each balloon.
Draw two more notes that follow
the direction of the arrow.

7

THE BASS CLEF SIGN 𝄢:
(The "F" Clef)

This sign comes from the old-fashioned letter F.

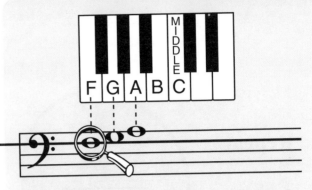

This is the F line ——————————————————

The F line passes between
the two dots of the **Bass Clef** sign.

You will usually play the low notes written
on the Bass Staff with your **left hand**.

The note F is your reading guide for the Bass Clef. You can name any note on the Bass Staff by moving up or down from the F line.

Hide And Seek

Mona Rejino

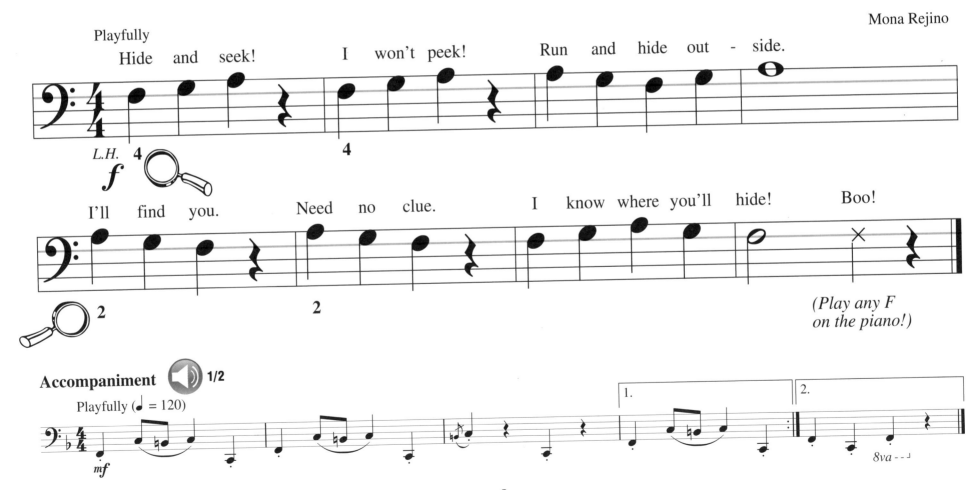

Playfully

Hide and seek!   I won't peek!   Run and hide out - side.

L.H. 4   *f*

I'll find you.   Need no clue.   I know where you'll hide!   Boo!

*(Play any F
on the piano!)*

Accompaniment 🔊 1/2

Playfully (♩ = 120)

mf

8va - - -

Whenever you see this magnifying glass, fill in the name of the note.

Title:_____

You already know how to play this song.
Do you know its name?

Bouncy  3/4

The Bass Clef
(F Clef)

Bass clefs are easy to make. Just follow Bear's instructions.
Trace each step and then draw your own Bass Clef.

1. **2.** **3.**

This is the F line. Colour it blue.

1. Colour each F line blue.
2. Draw a Bass Clef on each staff.
3. Draw the note F on each staff.

10

Notes On The Bass Staff

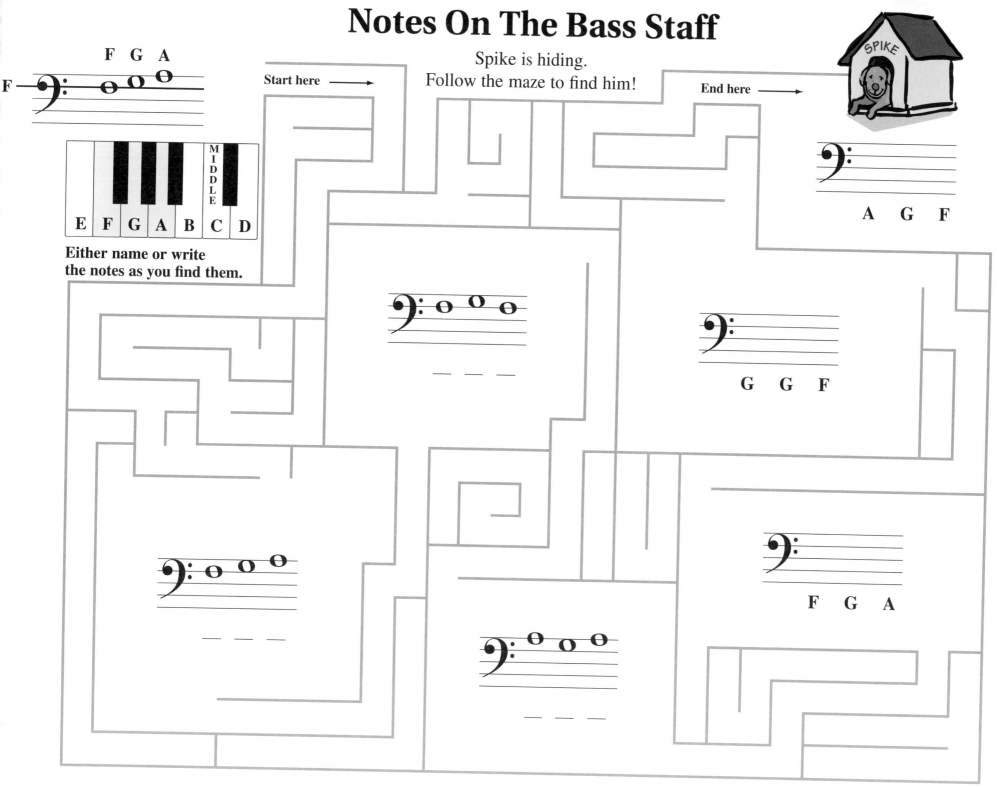

Spike is hiding.
Follow the maze to find him!

Either name or write
the notes as you find them.

THE TREBLE CLEF SIGN
(The "G" Clef)

This sign comes from the old-fashioned letter G.

This is the G line.

The G line passes through the curl of the **Treble Clef** sign.

You will usually play the high notes written on the Treble Staff with your **right hand**.

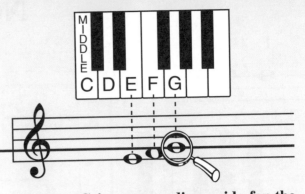

The note G is your reading guide for the Treble Clef. You can name any note on the Treble Staff by moving up or down from the G line.

Oh, Gee (G)

Music by Fred Kern
Words by Claire Berthold

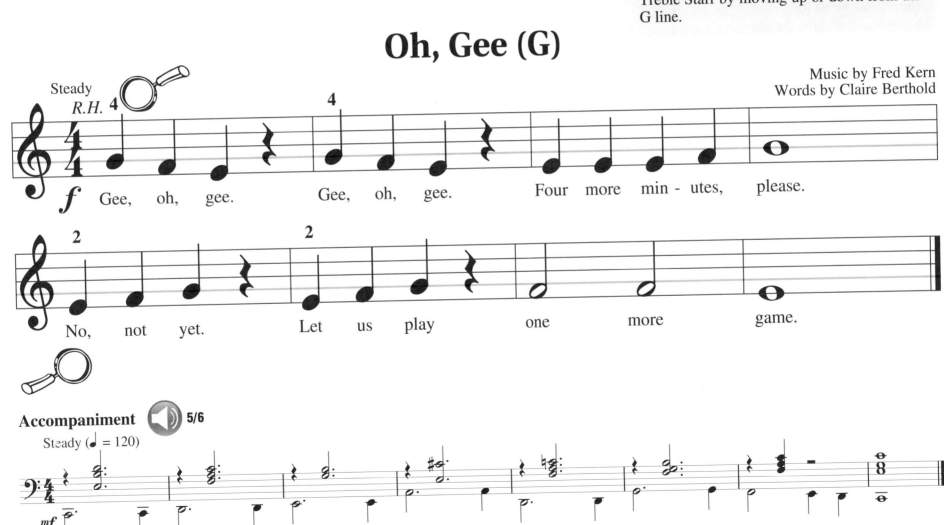

Steady
R.H. 4

Gee, oh, gee. Gee, oh, gee. Four more min - utes, please.

No, not yet. Let us play one more game.

Accompaniment 5/6

Steady (♩ = 120)

Hopscotch

Mona Rejino

Bouncy

R.H. **4**

𝆑 Hop - scotch on the walk. I won - der who will win.

5
2

Lines and spac - es drawn in chalk; now we can be - gin.

Accompaniment 🔊 7/8

Bouncy (♩ = 120)

mf

5

13

Treble Clef Sign
(G Clef)

If you follow Bear's instructions, you will make a treble clef.
Trace each step as you then draw your own.

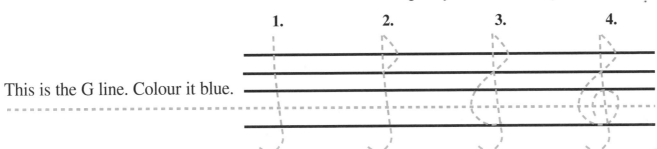

1.   **2.**   **3.**   **4.**

This is the G line. Colour it blue.

1. Colour each G line blue.
2. Draw a Treble Clef on each staff.
3. Draw the note G on each staff.

G

G

G

G

G

Notes On The Treble Staff

It's time for a game of hopscotch!

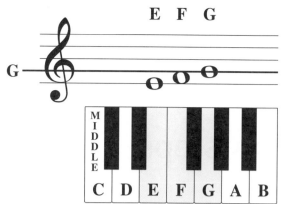

Either name or write the notes in each square.

Sneaky Footsteps

On tiptoe

Accompaniment (Student plays one octave higher than written.) 9/10

On tiptoe (♩=120)

16

THE GRAND STAFF
A Musical Map

The Bass Staff and the Treble Staff together make the **GRAND STAFF**, a Musical Map that tells you which key to play.

Middle C uses the short line (ledger line) between the Bass Staff and Treble Staff.

The Grand Staff – A Musical Map
(Activity Page)

Help Inspector Hound complete his map.

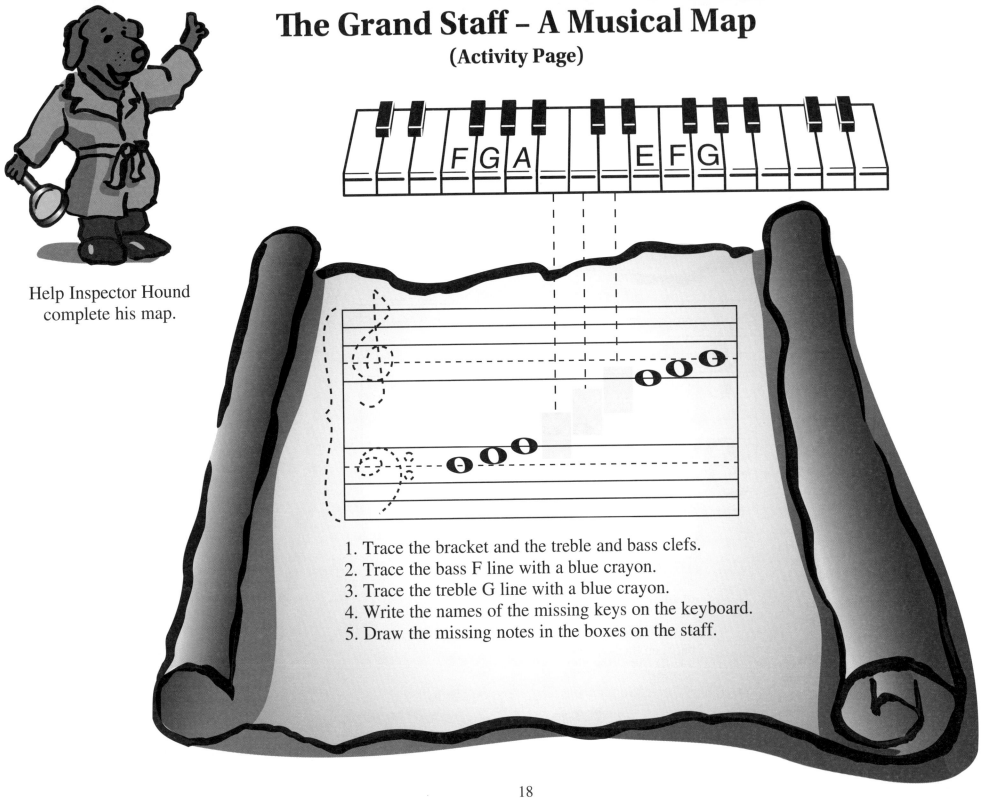

1. Trace the bracket and the treble and bass clefs.
2. Trace the bass F line with a blue crayon.
3. Trace the treble G line with a blue crayon.
4. Write the names of the missing keys on the keyboard.
5. Draw the missing notes in the boxes on the staff.

Thumbs share Middle C in this position.

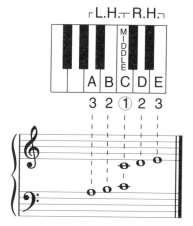

My Best Friend

"Pierrot"

Happily **11/12**

f My best friend is *Lind - say. We play ev - 'ry day.

Hey, we just got start - ed. I wish she could stay.

* Fill in the name of your own friend.

Notes Above and Below Middle C

Complete the stepping pattern for *Tambourine Tune*,
one of Party Cat's favourite melodies.

1. Draw the missing crotchet notes in the boxes.
2. In the second line, write the name of each note with a line above or below it.
3. Play the completed melody.

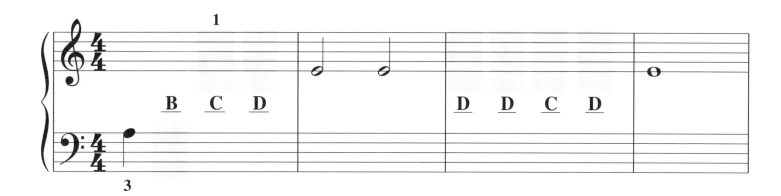

B   C   D   D   D   C   D

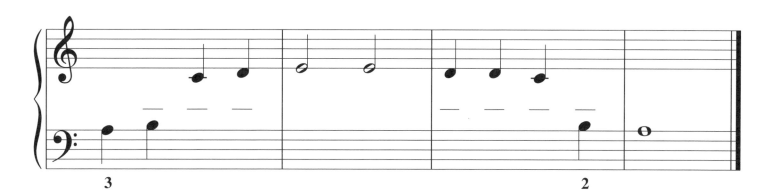

20

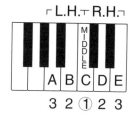

Tambourine Tune

With spirit

Folk Tune

Accompaniment (Student plays one octave higher than written.) 🔊 **13/14**

With spirit (♩ = 150)

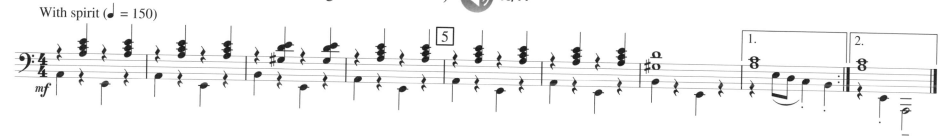

Read & Discover

Tambourine Tune
(Activity Page)

1. **Melody**

Write the names of the notes
in the boxes below the melody.

2. **Variation**

Vary the melody in *Tambourine Tune* by using the letter
names below. Write the notes on the staff using the same
rhythm.

E   E   D   C   B   A

3. Read the question and circle the correct answer.

   Which plays the alphabet going backward?   1. the melody   2. the variation

4. Play *Tambourine Tune* using the variation for bars 1-2 and 5-6.

Star To Star

Smoothly

p Smooth - ly glid - ing | in my dreams | through the moon - lit | night;

Float - ing down from | star to star. | Morn - ing ends this | flight.

Accompaniment (Student plays one octave higher than written.) 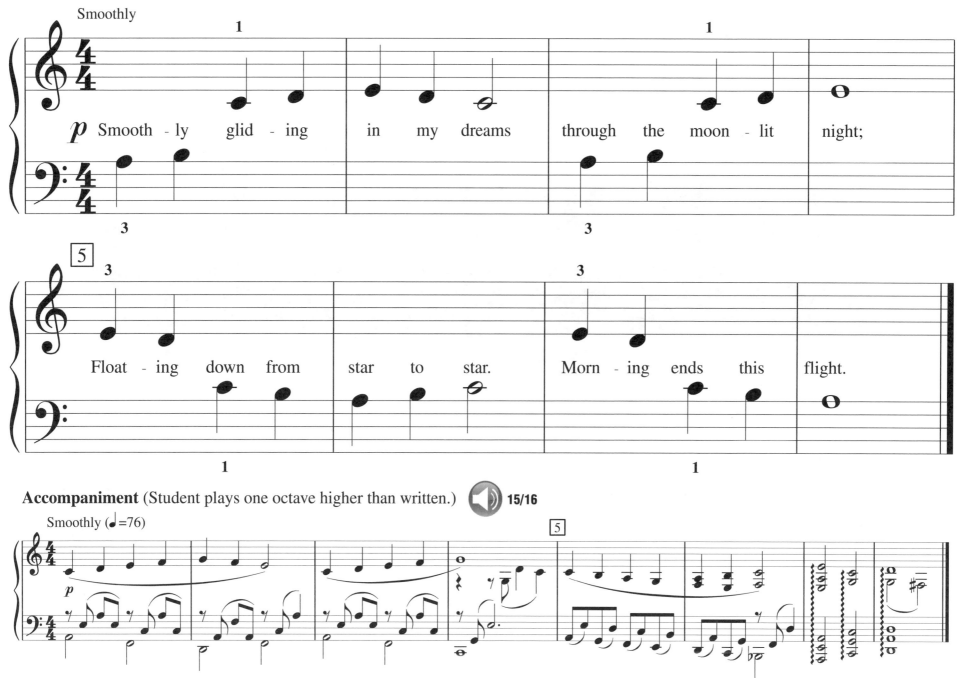 **15/16**

Smoothly (♩=76)

p

The Grand Staff Garden

Two inchworms found a surprise in *The Grand Staff Garden*.
Discover their names and what they found by completing the sentence below.

Write the name of each note in its blank in the sentence below.

___ ___ ___ and ___ ___ ate the ___ ___ ___ ___ ___ ___ ___.

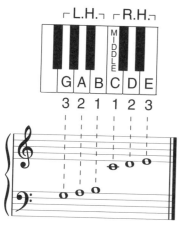

Once A Man Was So So Mad

Folk Tune

Steady

f
1. Once a man was so so mad, he jumped in - to a pa - per bag.
2. Pa - per bag, it was so thin, he jumped up - on a point - ed pin.

3. Pointed pin, it was so sharp,
   He jumped upon an Irish harp.

4. Irish harp, it was so pretty,
   He jumped upon a little kitty.

5. Little kitty began to scratch,
   He jumped into a cabbage patch.

6. Cabbage patch, it was so big,
   He jumped upon a big fat pig.

7. Big fat pig began to tickle,
   He jumped upon a big dill pickle.

8. Big dill pickle was so sour,
   He jumped upon a big sunflower.

9. Bee came by and stung his chin, and
   That's the last I've heard of him!

Accompaniment (Student plays one octave higher than written.) 🔊 17/18

Steady
(♩ = 130)
mf
1-8.
Last time

25

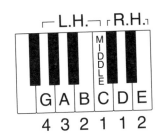

Wishful Thinking

Mona Rejino

Smoothly

Some day, some - where, I will make my wish come true.

Some - time, some place, if I fol - low through.

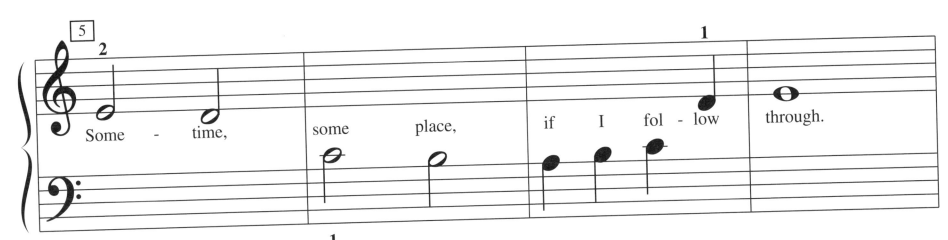

19/20

Accompaniment (Student plays one octave higher than written.)

Smoothly (♩ = 105)

p
With pedal

26

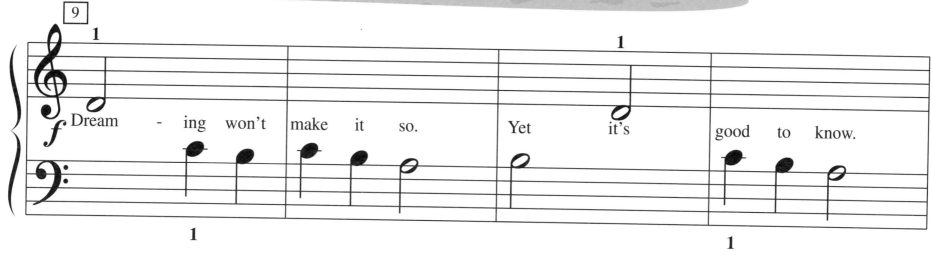

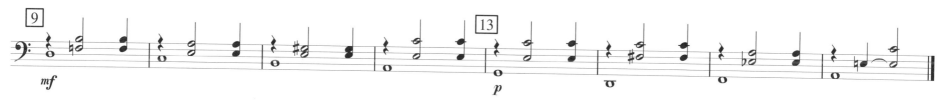

27

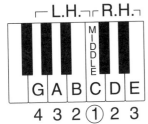

Toes In The Sand

This song can be expanded by improvising on A B C D E as shown on the next page!

Phillip Keveren

Relaxed

Toes   in   the   sand   be - neath   the   tur - quoise   sky.

Build - ing   a   cas - tle,   gen - tle   waves   wash   by.

21/22

Accompaniment (Student plays one octave higher than written.)

Relaxed (♩ = 120)

Continue to next page for improvisation.

Keep your hands in the A B C D E position.

Listen and feel the pulse as your teacher plays the accompaniment below. When you are ready, make up your own song by mixing the notes in any order you want.

Play the eight-bar melody on page 28, improvise a bit on page 29, then return to the main melody (the "head" in jazz slang) at the beginning of the piece.

Repeat ad lib.

Student returns to head.

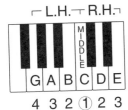

Long, Long Ago

Thomas Haynes Bailey

Accompaniment (Student plays two octaves higher than written.) 23/24

MEZZO PIANO

mp

means moderately soft

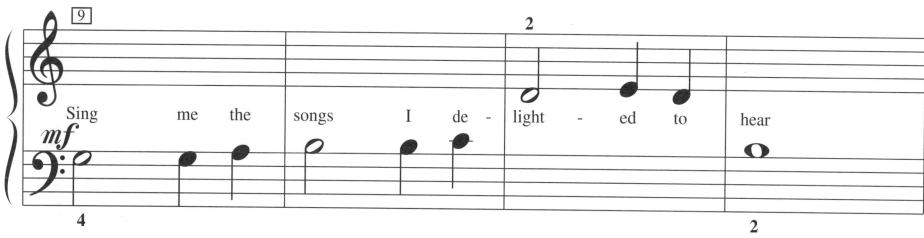

Sing me the songs I de - light - ed to hear

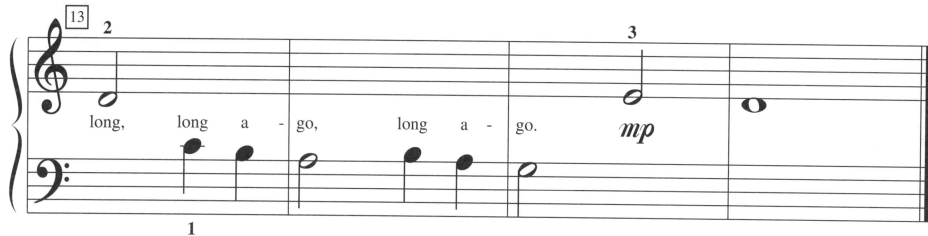

long, long a - go, long a - go. *mp*

31

Long, Long Ago
(Activity Page)

Let's go on a Bar Hunt!

These rhythms appear in *Long, Long Ago*. Study the score on pages 30–31 and count how many times you play each pattern. Write your answers in the boxes below.

Imagine & Create

Place your hands in the *Long, Long Ago* position.
Improvise a new piece as your teacher plays the accompaniment below.

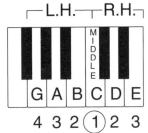

Accompaniment

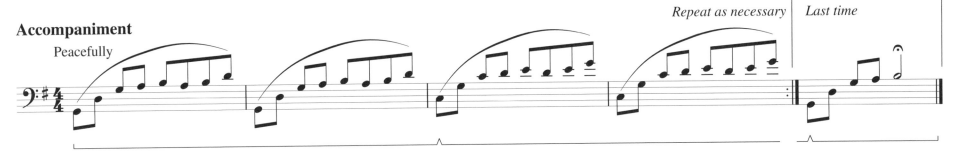

From *Soft* To LOUD

Listen as your teacher plays *Tambourine Tune* (on page 21) two different times.
Circle the sign that matches the sound of the music each time you hear it.

Arrange the dynamic signs above from soft to loud in the boxes below.

Now arrange the signs from loud to soft.

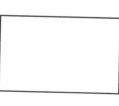

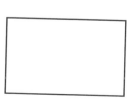

Whistling Tune

Fred Kern

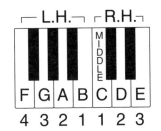

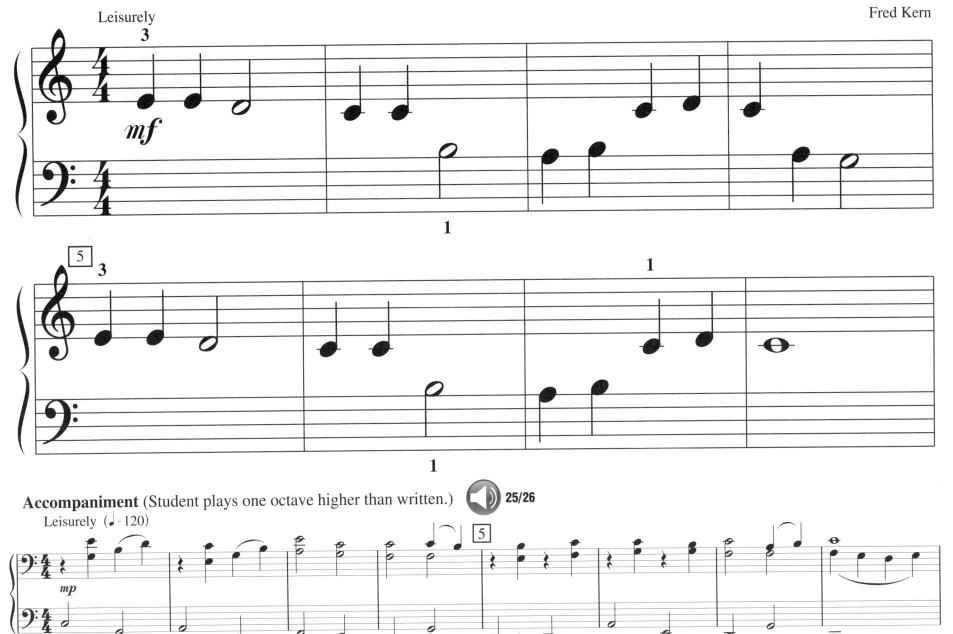

Accompaniment (Student plays one octave higher than written.) 🔊 **25/26**

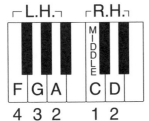

Struttin'

Mona Rejino

Steady

mf Do you feel like strut - tin' when things go your way?

Pea - nut but - ter waf - fles real - ly make my day!

Accompaniment (Student plays one octave higher than written.) 27/28

Steady (♩ = 135)

mp

36

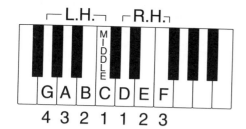

Old Saw*

Fred Kern

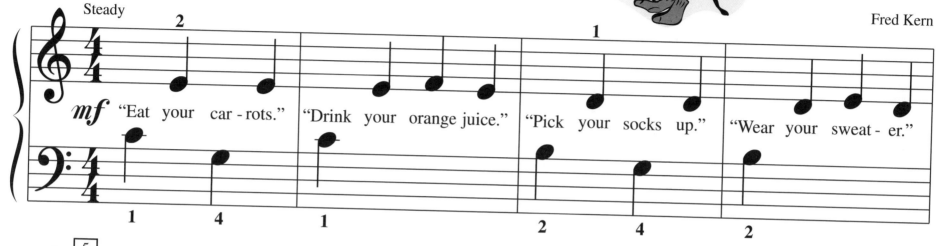

Steady

mf "Eat your car-rots." "Drink your orange juice." "Pick your socks up." "Wear your sweat-er."

"Close the door." "Don't bring that mud in." "Brush your teeth." "Now go to bed."

An old "saw" is a saying used so often that it becomes commonplace.

Accompaniment (Student plays one octave higher than written.) 🔊 **29/30**

Steady (♩=130)

mp

Nobody Knows
The Trouble I'm In

Barbara Kreader

Playfully

mp No - bod - y knows the trou - ble I'm in.

No - bod - y knows but my friend An - drew.

Accompaniment (Student plays one octave higher than written.) 🔊 **31/32**

Playfully (♩ = 180)

p

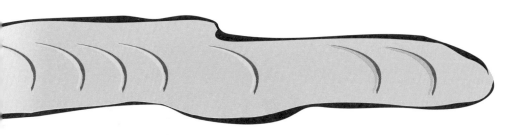

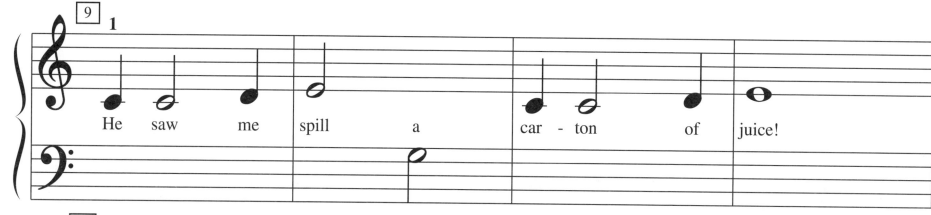

He saw me spill a car - ton of juice!

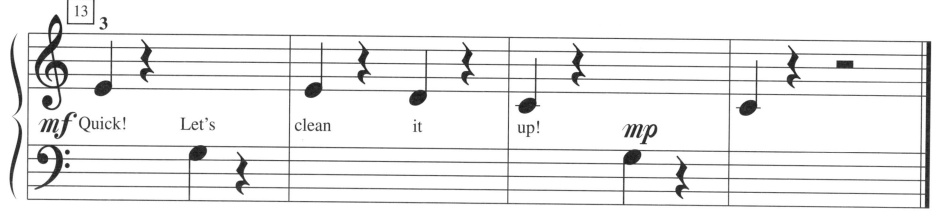

mf Quick! Let's clean it up! *mp*

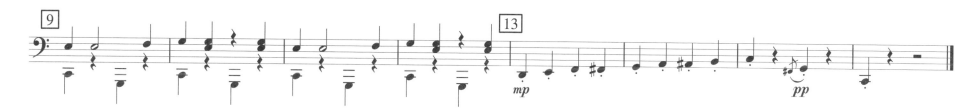

Nobody Knows
The Trouble I'm In
(Activity Page)

Go to the score of *Nobody Knows The Trouble I'm In* on pages 38–39.
Match the rhythm of the words in column A to the rhythm of the notes
in column B by drawing a line from column A to column B.

(Hint: One of the rhythms listed in column B will be used more than once.)

A   **B**

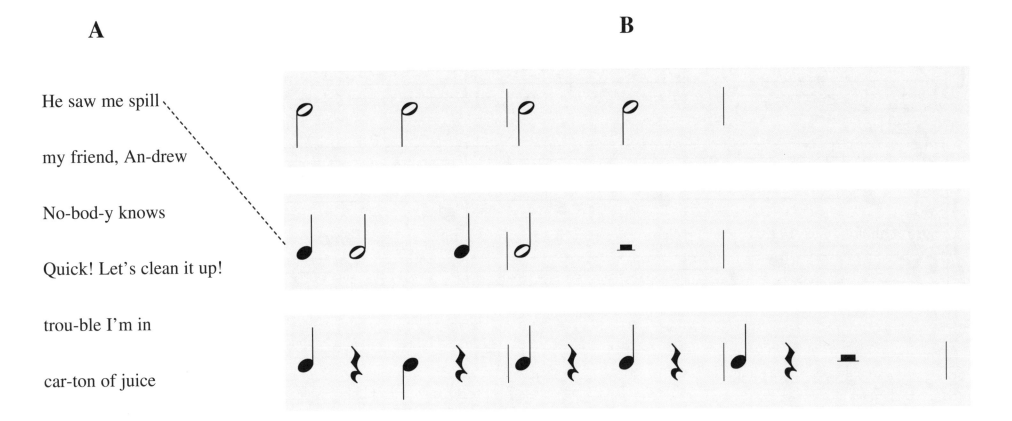

He saw me spill

my friend, An-drew

No-bod-y knows

Quick! Let's clean it up!

trou-ble I'm in

car-ton of juice

Who Could It Be?

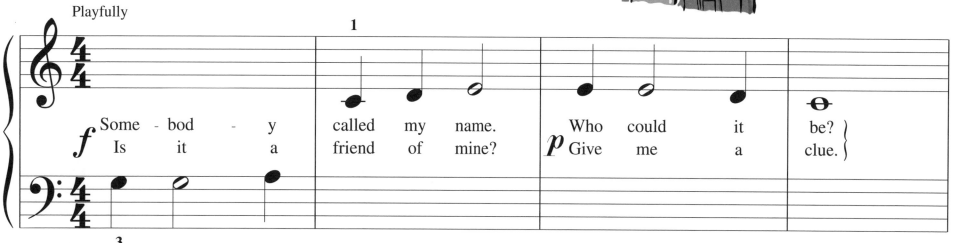

Playfully

f Some - bod - y called my name. **p** Who could it be?
Is it a friend of mine? Give me a clue.

f Sure hope that it was you!

Accompaniment (Student plays two octaves higher than written.) 33/34

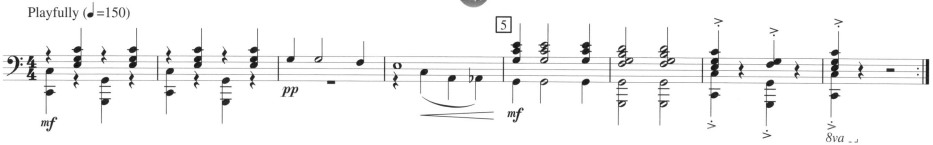

Playfully (♩=150)

mf   *pp*   *mf*

8va

SKIPS
(3rds)

On the Piano, a 3rd
- skips a key
- skips a finger
- skips a letter

On the Staff, a 3rd skips a letter from either
- line to line or
- space to space

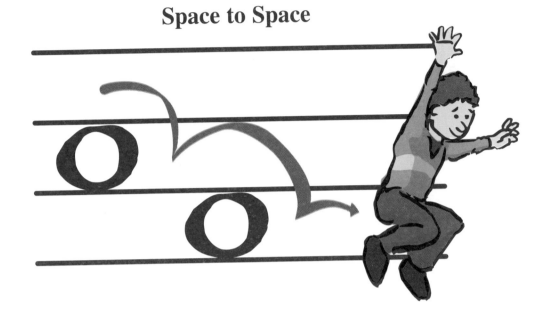

Space to Space

Skip down
(3rd)

Line to Line

Skip up
(3rd)

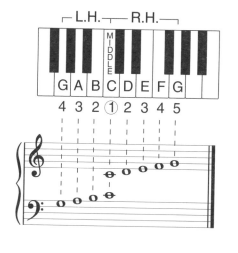

Lively  35/36

Surprise Symphony

Joseph Haydn
(1732 - 1809)

Skips (3rds)
(Activity Page)

Match each skip on the staff to the same skip on the
keyboard by drawing a line from Column A to Column B.

A

B

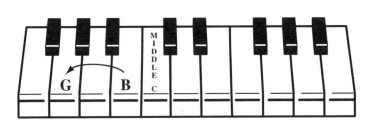

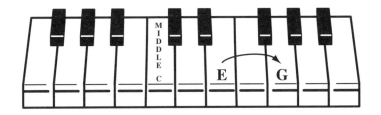

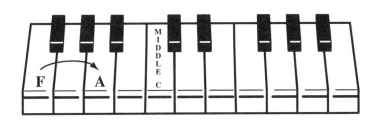

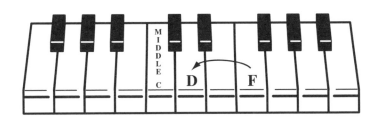

Surprise Symphony
(Activity Page)

Skips (3rds)

1. Study these bars from *Surprise Symphony*.

   Write the name of the note in the magnifying glass.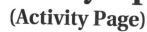
   Show the direction of the melody in the boxes.

2. Complete these sentences by circling the correct ending.   (circle one)

   The skips in bars 1 and 2 go from: **line to line** or **space to space**.

   The skips in bars 3 and 4 go from: **line to line** or **space to space**.

Dreaming And Drifting

Gently rocking

Accompaniment (Student plays two octaves higher than written.) 🔊 **37/38**

Gently rocking (♩=80)

p

With pedal

Happy Heart

Accompaniment (Student plays one octave higher than written.) 🔊 **39/40**

47

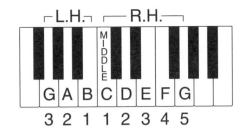

By The River's Edge

Carol Klose

Quietly flowing along

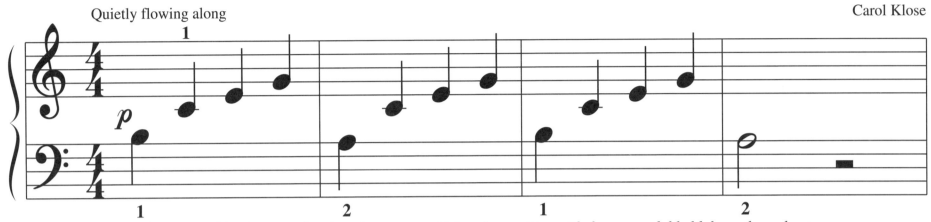

For solo performance, this piece may be played one octave higher than written with damper pedal held down throughout.

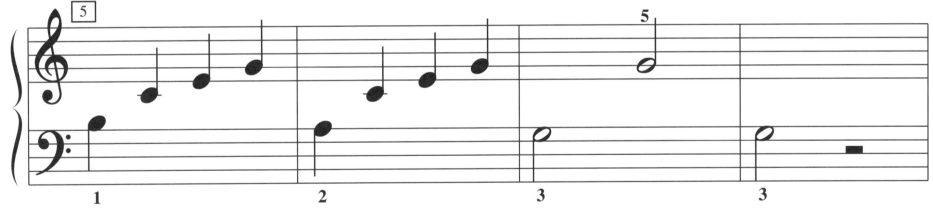

Accompaniment (Student plays two octaves higher than written.) 🔊 **41/42**

Quietly flowing along (♩=120)

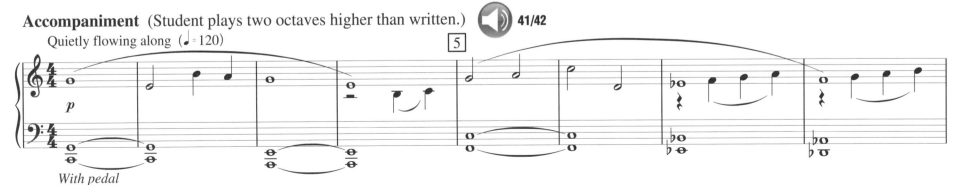

With pedal

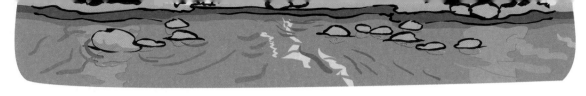

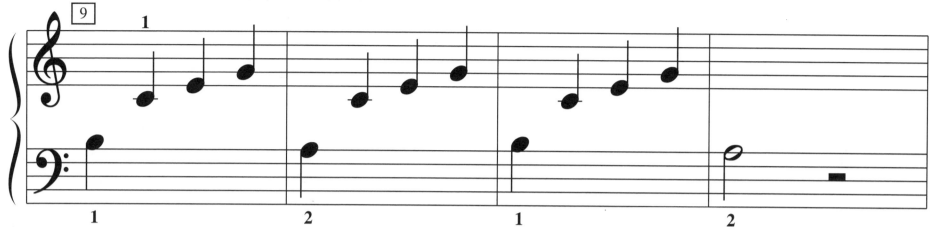

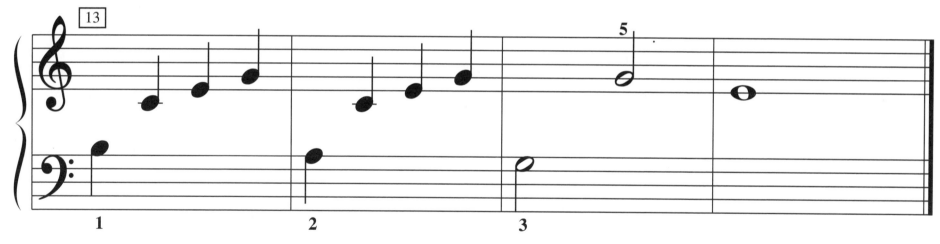

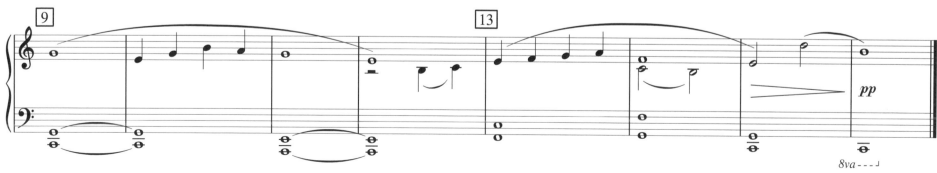

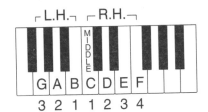

Skateboard Doodle

"Yankee Doodle"

With energy

f Once my broth - er   sped down -town,   rid - ing   on his   skate -   board.

Took   a   curve   and   lost   his   nerve   and   turned in - to   a   trash   can.

43/44

Accompaniment (Student plays one octave higher than written.)

With energy
(♩ = 130)

mf

R.H. over L.H.

8va -

50

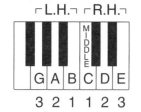

Let Me Fly!

Smoothly

Spiritual

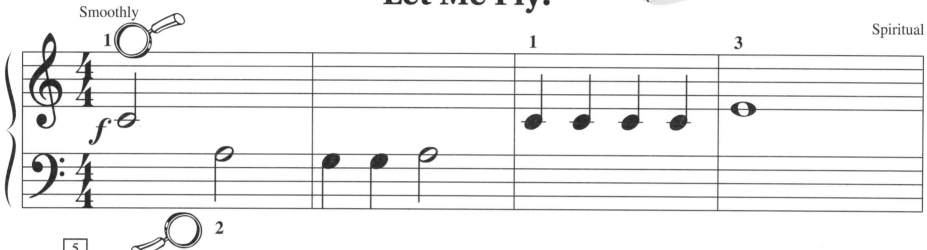

Accompaniment (Student plays one octave higher than written.) 45/46

Smoothly (♩ = 120)

With pedal

51

More Steps

Fill each of Party Cat's balloons with three semibreve notes that **step** higher or lower.
Use the arrows as a guide.

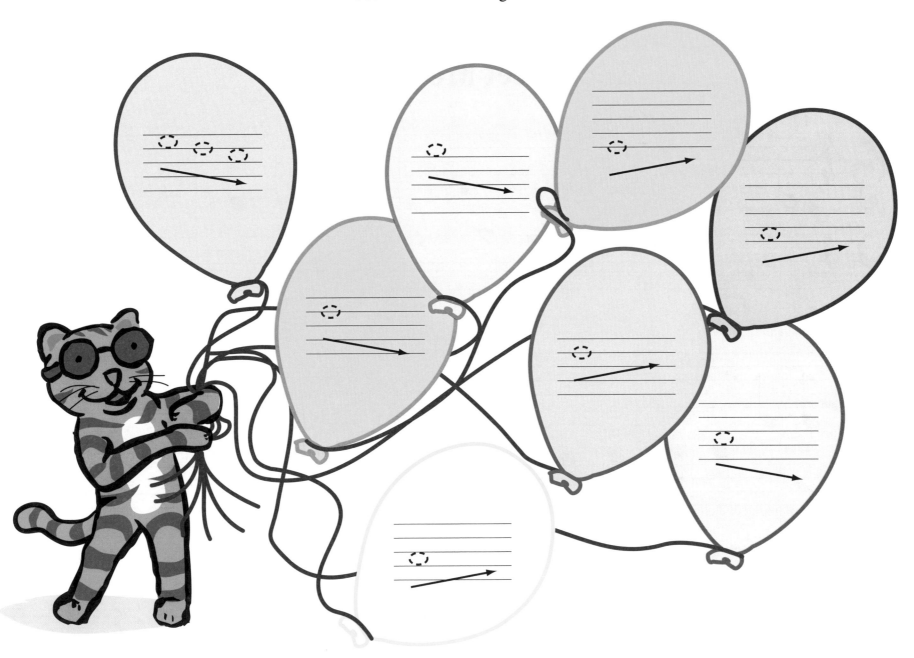

More Skips

Fill each of Spike's balloons with three
semibreve notes that **skip** higher or lower.
Use the arrows as a guide.

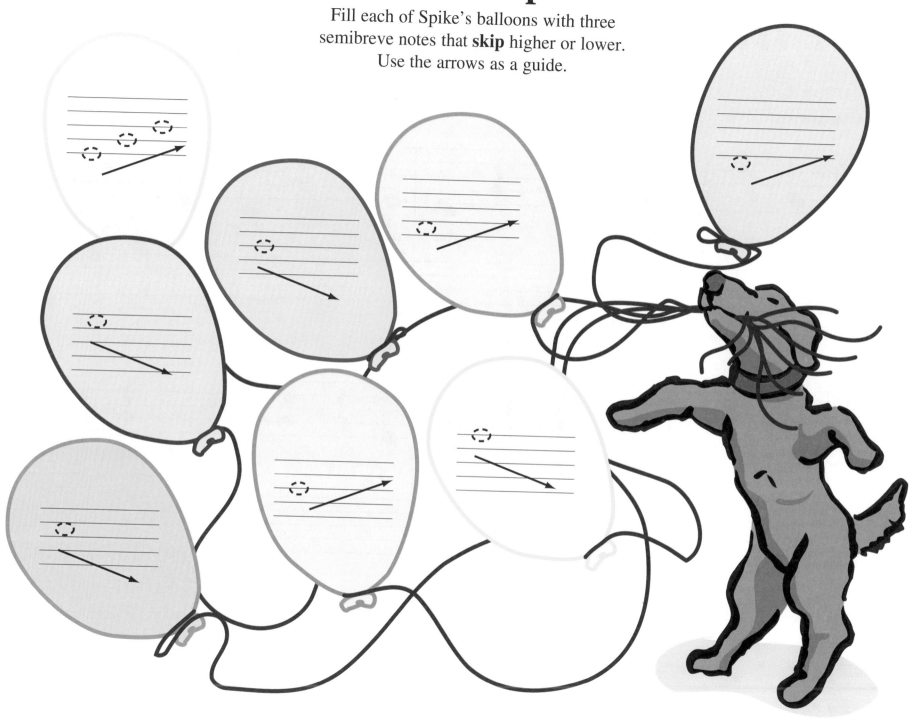

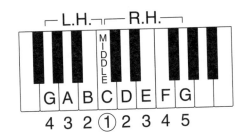

The Wild Rest

Bill Boyd

Moderately

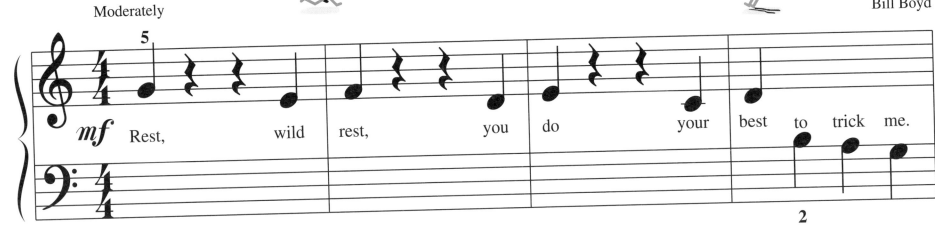

Rest, wild rest, you do your best to trick me.

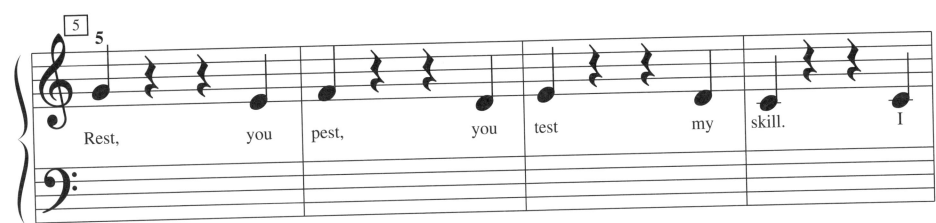

Rest, you pest, you test my skill. I

Accompaniment (Student plays one octave higher than written.) 🔊 **47/48**

Moderately (♪♪ = ♪ ³ ♪) (♩ = 140)

54

count and count a - gain, but you're al - ways chang - ing meas - ures on me.

Rest, wild rest, don't jest, be still.

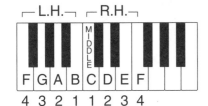

Star Quest

Phillip Keveren

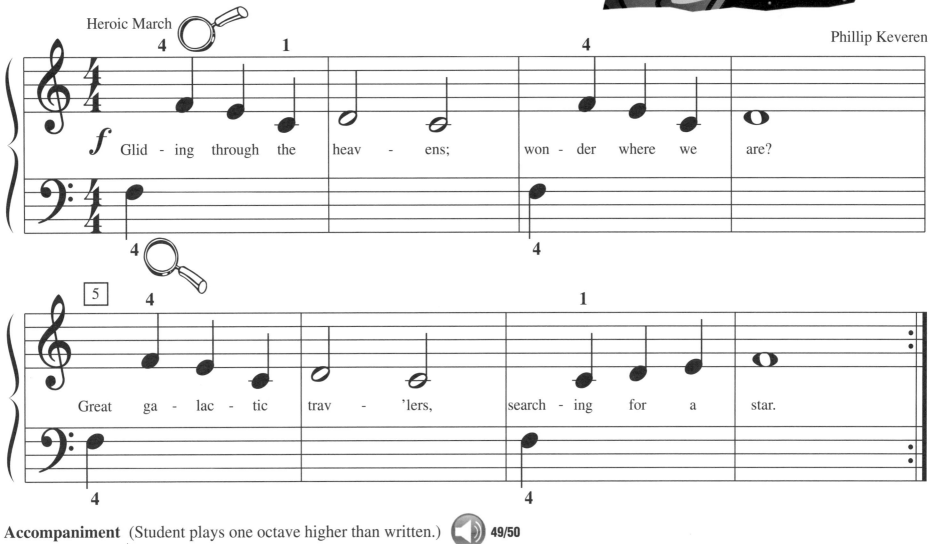

Heroic March

Glid - ing through the heav - ens; won - der where we are?

Great ga - lac - tic trav - 'lers, search - ing for a star.

Accompaniment (Student plays one octave higher than written.) 49/50

Heroic March (♩ = 120)

56

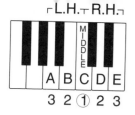

L.H. R.H.

A B C D E
3 2 ① 2 3

Solemn Event

Italo Taranta

Accompaniment (Student plays one octave higher than written.) 🔊 51/52

Adagio (♩ = 80)

Read & Discover

🔊 52

Solemn Event
(Activity Page)

Reading Warm-up

1. Write the name of the note in the magnifying glasses and then draw an arrow to show the direction of the melody.

Step Up (2nd) ↗

Step Down (2nd) ↘

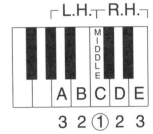

L.H. R.H.

A B C D E

3 2 ① 2 3

2. As you listen to the accompaniment to *Solemn Event*, play this warm-up in an *Adagio* (slow) tempo three octaves higher than written.

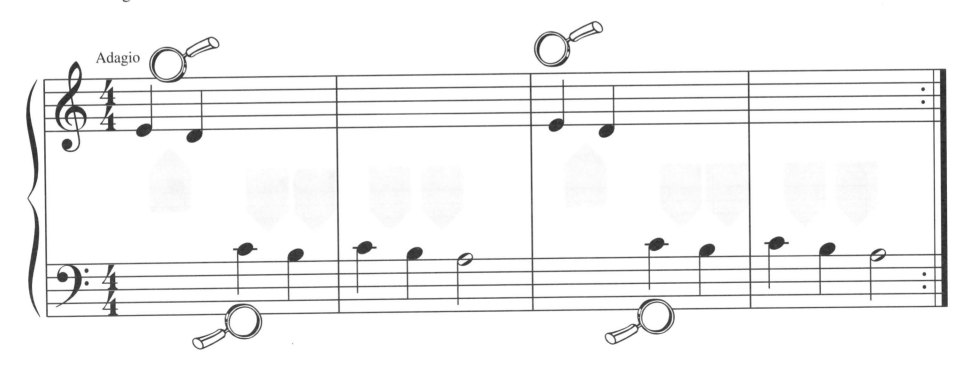

Up To Tempo!

Tempo marks tell the mood of the music and the speed of the piece.

Circle the picture that describes the tempo marking.

Adagio

Allegro

Andante

Your teacher will play three examples.
Circle the tempo mark that fits the speed and mood of the music.

1.
Adagio

Andante

Allegro

2.
Adagio

Andante

Allegro

3.
Adagio

Andante

Allegro

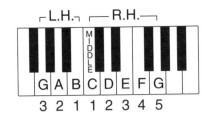

D.C. (Da Capo) al Fine

When you see this sign, return to the beginning (capo) of the piece and play until you see the sign for the end (fine).

I Like You!

53/54

Allegro

Folk Tune

Fine

mf

I   like   you!   You're my own best   friend.

Laugh - ing with me   when I'm hap - py,   stand - ing   by   me   when I'm crab - by,

D.C. al Fine

60

Just Being Me!

Czechoslovakian

Lively

mf Run - ning, skip - ping, jump - ing, and hop - ping, and hum - ming, sing - ing, flip - ping, and

flop - ping. I'm hap - py to be *El - lie, I'm El - lie. I'm hap - py to be me!

*Fill in your own name.

Accompaniment (Student plays one octave higher than written.)

Lively
(♩ = 150)

mp

Steps or Skips?

In *Just Being Me!* some bars have steps and others have skips.
Study the score again and circle the word that completes each sentence below.

(circle one)

1. In the bars that use the rhythm  the music moves by: **steps** or **skips.**

2. In the bars that use the rhythm  the music moves by: **steps** or **skips.**

Imagine & Create

Just Being Me!
(Activity Page)

Put the pieces back together!

1. Cut out the cards on the next page.

   Begin with the clef signs and add the time signature.

   Arrange the groups of notes in the order they appear in *Just Being Me!*

2. Play the piece to see if you put the notes in the correct order.

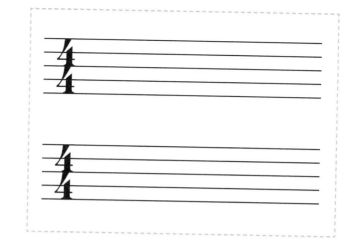

Trumpet Man

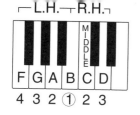

DOTTED MINIM NOTE

A **Dotted Minim Note** fills the time of three crotchet notes.

= 3 beats

= 3 beats

Count: "1 2 3"
clap - hold - hold

"Camptown Races"

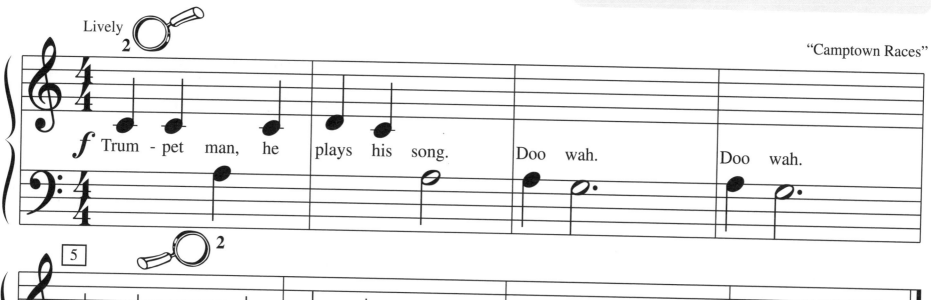

Trum - pet man, he plays his song. Doo wah. Doo wah.

Asks us all to sing a - long. Oh, doo wah day.

Accompaniment (Student plays one octave higher than written.) 57/58

Lively (♩ = 160)

The Dotted Minim Note

A dotted minim note equals 3 beats.

Play the first two bars of *Camptown Races (Trumpet Man)*.

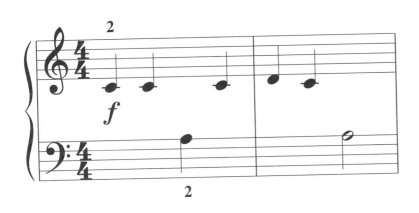

Your teacher will complete the first line of the song by playing one of the examples below.
Circle the example your teacher plays.

1.

2.

3.

Now play the first four bars of *Camptown Races*.

TIME SIGNATURE

3/4 (3/♩) = three beats fill every bar
= crotchet note gets one beat

Scottish Air

Folk Tune

Andante

mf Slide and step and turn to the mu - sic. The

bag - pipes are dron - ing. A song's in the air.

Accompaniment (Student plays one octave higher than written.) 🔊 **59/60**

Andante (♩ = 145)

mp

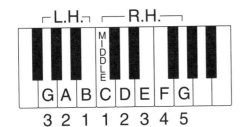

The Step Waltz

Phillip Keveren

Allegretto

mf This lit - tle | waltz real - ly | wrote it - self

step - by - | step in a | day - | dream.

Accompaniment (Student plays two octaves higher than written.) 🔊 **61/62**

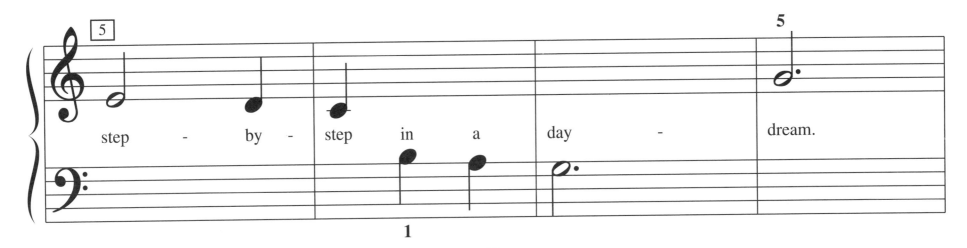

Allegretto (♩= 145)

mp

Note next to note it's no sym - pho - ny, but it's

per - fect for whist - ling or sing - ing.

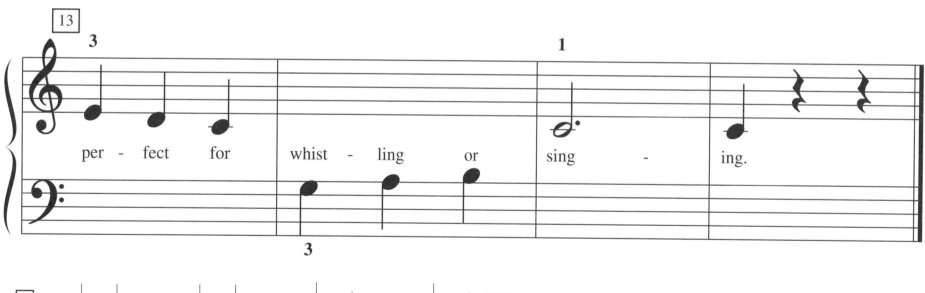

69

$\frac{3}{4}$ or $\frac{4}{4}$?

Bear wrote down some of his favourite songs,
but he forgot the time signatures.

1. Write the correct time signature in the box at the beginning of each piece.
2. Play each melody.

Pop, Goes The Weasel

Surprise Symphony

Home, Home On The Range

Yankee Doodle

Rhythm Jam

Party Cat is practising for his next piano lesson.
Help him count the rhythm in his new pieces.

1. Circle the note or rest in the blue box that will complete
   the rhythm in each bar.
2. Clap and count each example.

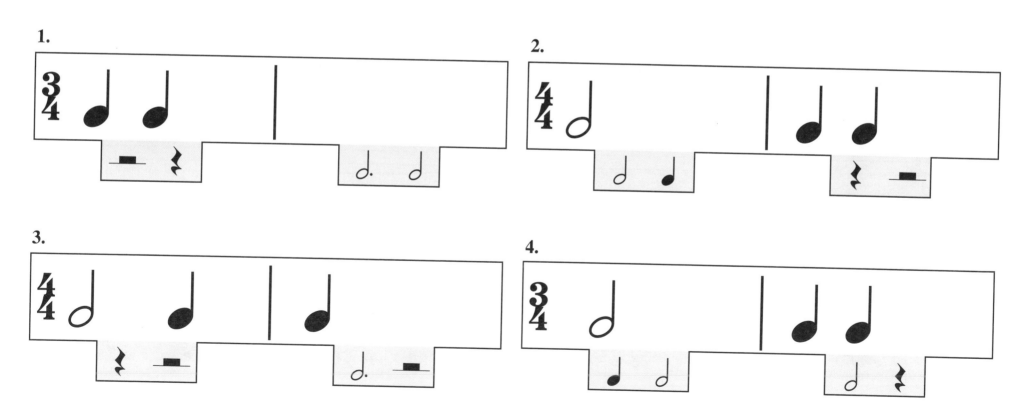

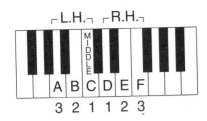

Pirates Of The Sea

Janet Feldman

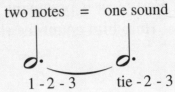

Boldly

mp Sail - ing ships to far - a - way plac - es, where

treas - ure waits for me!

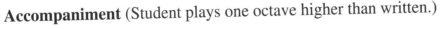

Accompaniment (Student plays one octave higher than written.) 🔊 **63/64**

Boldly (♩ = 150)

p

9 3

mf Friend   or   foe,   we   sing,   Yo   Ho!   We're   the

1

13 1

Pi - rates   of   the   Sea! _____

1

9

mp

13

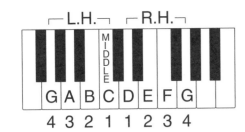

Hard As A Rock

Bill Boyd

Accompaniment (Student plays one octave higher than written.) 🔊 **65/66**

Relay Review

Spike and Party Cat are racing to finish their theory workbook.
Match the correct answers by drawing a line from Column A to Column B.
Record your time in the box at the end of each race.

START

A	B
	moderately soft
mp	crotchet rest = 1 beat
	repeated notes
4/4	Four beats fill every bar. ♩ gets one beat.
	minim note = 2 beats
f	steps (2nds)
𝄽	loud
♩	crotchet note = 1 beat

START

A	B
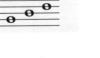	soft
	tie
	moderately loud
p	three beats fill every bar. ♩ gets one beat.
	dotted minim note = 3 beats
mf	semibreve note = 4 beats
	minim rest = 2 beats
	skips (3rds)

The winner is:

_____

FINISH   Seconds

FINISH   Seconds

Go For The Gold
(Activity Page)

Before athletes "Go For The Gold," they spend long hours warming up, analyzing their moves, and practising. The same is true for musicians.

 67

As you listen to *Go For The Gold,* tap and count this rhythm. Remember to give the first beat of every bar extra emphasis.

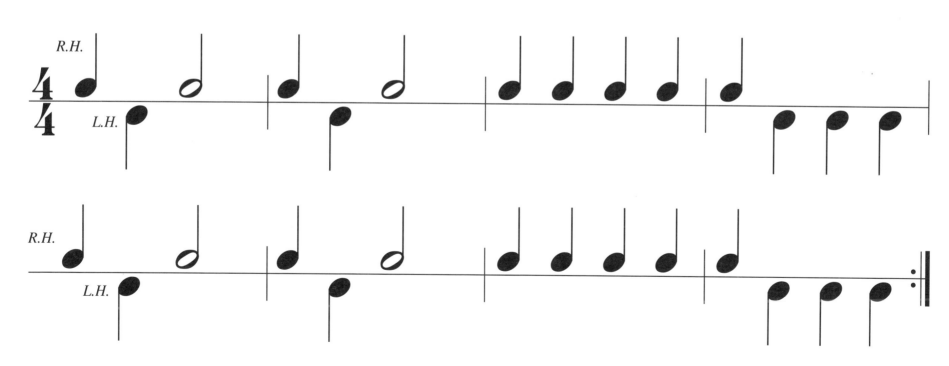

Go For The Gold

Phillip Keveren

Accompaniment (Student plays one octave higher than written.) 🔊 **67/68**

AWARD CERTIFICATE

HAS SUCCESSFULLY COMPLETED
HAL LEONARD ALL-IN-ONE
PIANO LESSONS, BOOK B
AND
IS HEREBY PROMOTED TO
BOOK TWO

_____   _____
TEACHER   DATE

HAL•LEONARD®

All-In-One
Piano Lessons
Book B

GOLD
AWARD
MEDAL

HAL•LEONARD®

Cut-out may be fitted over student's shirt button.